Also by Kim Gaddy:

Story Time:
Picture Quilts to Stir a Child's Imagination
(2012)

Available at PickleDishStore.com,
Kansas City Star Quilts online

Farm-Fresh Quilts

Simple Projects Inspired by the Simple Life

✳ By Kim Gaddy ✳

KANSAS CITY STAR
QUILTS
Continuing the Tradition

Farm-Fresh Quilts
Simple Projects Inspired by the Simple Life

By Kim Gaddy
Edited by Judy Pearlstein
Technical Edit by Nan Doljac
Design by Amy Robertson
Photographs by Aaron Leimkuehler
Illustrations by Lon Eric Craven
Production Assistance by Jo Ann Groves

Published by Kansas City Star Books
1729 Grand Boulevard
Kansas City, Missouri 64108

First edition, first printing
ISBN: 2013933475
Library of Congress number: 978-1-61169-089-7

Printed in the United States of America
By Walsworth Publishing Co.
Marceline, Missouri

To order copies, call StarInfo, 816-234-4242. (Say "Operator.")

Contents

About the Author

Four years ago my husband and I decided we wanted to simplify our lives. We bought five acres just outside of Austin, Texas, from my grandmother and moved our family into the charming 1860s stone house on the property. One large garden, a few bee hives, two goats, two cows, four pigs, three dogs, several guineas and innumerable chickens later, I'm not quite sure we managed to simplify our lives, but I wouldn't have it any other way.

The quilts in this book were inspired by the best of daily life around our place. I hope as you look through the projects and start one of your own, you find a little slice of country simplicity.

Many thanks to the accomplished quilters who helped me work on these projects. Osie Lebowitz,

Debbie Balagia, Connie McKay and Shirley Heart helped me sew and provided much appreciated guidance and encouragement. As usual, long arm quilter Angela McCorkle made my patchwork shine with her beautiful quilting. Thanks to you all.

And thanks to my parents — to my father for teaching me to garden and to my mother for teaching me to sew. And to both for teaching me to appreciate the simple things in life. What better life lesson could there be?

Wishing you all many happy hours sewing, gardening, and spending time with friends and family!

—Kim

Acknowledgments

This book is easy to follow and a pleasure to browse through due to the talents of Judy Pearlstein, Amy Robertson, Lon Eric Craven, Aaron Leimkuehler and Nan Doljac. Thank you for such a beautiful setting in which to place my quilts.

Simple Life

40" x 58" ✷ By Kim Gaddy

CUTTING

Note that all dimensions given are finished dimensions. The instructions for individual blocks are included throughout this book as they take center stage in separate projects. See the quilt photo on page 11 for appliqué placement ideas. Embellish with buttons and embroidery after the quilt is quilted.

WOOL LETTERING

1. Start with well shrunken wool, wool felt, or felt. You want to make sure it isn't prone to unraveling and is colorfast.

2. With a rotary cutter, cut narrow strips of wool along the bias. I shoot for just a hair over ⅛" wide. You will be piecing the lettering so the wool strips don't have to be especially long. I usually cut strips of 6 to 8 inches.

3. Trace the words onto your background fabric.

4. Place dots of fabric glue along one stroke of the first letter of the word. Lay a wool strip along the glue and nudge it into place. Continue gluing and laying down the wool until you get to a natural end of the letter stroke and then trim the excess wool away. Start the process again. A single letter may be made from more than one continuous strip of wool. For example an "a" would have two strips of wool: the curved part on the left and the straight line on the right.

5. With matching thread and a zigzag stitch (set just wide enough to catch both edges of the wool—about ⅛" wide), sew the wool letters into place. Sew right down the center of the wool strip. Any wool not caught in the stitching should not unravel if it is washed, worsted or felted, but if you're concerned about a spot, simply put a dab of Fraycheck on it.

FABRIC

- 2⅔ yards ivory
- ⅔ yard yellow dot
- ⅓ yard green
- ¼ yard orange
- ⅓ yard gray check
- ¼ yard black
- ¼ yard strawberry
- Fat quarter house red
- ¼ yard black felted wool
- Less than ⅛ yard of the following colors: turquoise, blue, deep orange, dark yellow, medium yellow, light yellow, purple, light purple, dark pink, light pink, tomato red, grey, brown, light brown, various colors of bee skep gold-browns, orange felted wool for chick legs and beaks
- ½ yard for binding

WHERE TO FIND BLOCK INSTRUCTIONS

Finished Sizes

Churn Dash Block

½″x7⅛″ · ½″x7⅛″

Farm Animals — 5″x½″ — **Lettering** — 5″x½″
9″x5¾″ · 2¼″x5¾″ · Blocks: 1¼″x1¼″

Simplicity

15¼″x5¾″

15¼″x1¼″

Strawberry block · 1″x7″

5″x½″

Vegetables · **Hen and Chicks block** · **House Block** · **Pinwheel block**

6″x¾″ · 3″x3″ · 6″x¾″ · 6″x¾″
½″x20¼″

5″x1¾″ · 2″x1″ · 2″x1″ · 5″x1¼″ · 2″x1″ · 2″x1″ · 5″x2″ · 5″x¾″
½″x20¼″

3″x2″ · 6″x3″ · 3″x2″ · 2″x1″ · 2″x1″ · 2″x12″ · 2″x12″ · ½″ x 20¼″
12″x1¼″
4″x4″ · 4″x4″

Basket block · **Cherry block**

5″x1″ · 1¾″x1″ · 2″x1″ · 5″x1″ · ½″x4 · ½″x4 · ½″x4 · ½″x4 · ½″x6 · 5″x1″ · 5″x1″

Pumpkin block

6″x1″ · 5″x2″ · 8½″x6″ · 1″x7¼″ · 5″x¾″ · 1″x8¼″ · 8½″x2¼″ · 15½″x1″

4″x1″ · 2″x1″ · 2″x1″ · 1¼″x 5″ · 2″x1″ · 2″x1″ · ¼″x 5″

Bee Skep block

5″x½″

Gratitude

12½″x5¾″
12½″x1¼″
5″x½″

Hen and Chicks block

5″x1″ · 5″x1″ · 5″x1″ · 5″x1″ · 6″x3½″ · 5″x1″ · 1¾″x1″ · 2″x1″ · 1″x5″ · 1″x3½″ · 1″x3½″ · 1″x5″ · 1″x7″ · 4″x1″ · 2″x1″ · 2″x1″ · 4″x1″ · 5″x1½″ · 17″x1½″ · ½″ x15½″

5″x½″

4½″x1¾″ · 12½″x5¾″ · 4½″x¾″

Kindness

12½″x1¼″
5″x½″

9-Patch block
12¼″x8½″ · 3¾″x¼″ · 3¾″x¼″ · 1″x8½″ · ½″x8½″ · 3¾″x½″ · 3¾″x¼″

½″x7⅛″ · ½″x7⅛″

Churn Dash Quilt

50" x 57" ✳ By Kim Gaddy

Try this easy-to-piece quilt in fun, funky colors or in a more traditional colorway.

CUTTING GUIDE

For Churn Dash Blocks:

- 224 – 2" x 1¼" rectangles, dark fabric
- 224 – 2" x 1¼" rectangles, ivory fabric
- 56 – 2" ivory squares
- 112 – 3" squares ivory
- 112 – 3" squares dark

For Setting Squares:

- 72 – 6" squares of coordinating fabric

CHURN DASH BLOCK

1. Sew 56 Churn Dash blocks:

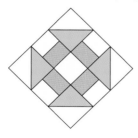

✳ For each block, use an ivory fabric and a darker fabric to sew four half-square triangles. Use your favorite method to sew the half-square triangles, or see Hen and Chick block on page 78. They should measure 2" square.

FABRIC

- 1 yard darker HST (half-square triangle) fabric or six fat quarters
- ½ yard gray fabric for 2" x 1¼" rectangles (gray rectangles on quilt chart)
- 1½ yards ivory
- 2¼ yards coordinating fabric for setting squares
- ½ yard for binding

2. Piece connecting units:

❊ For each churn dash square, cut four ivory 1¼" x 2" rectangles and four darker 1¼" x 2" rectangles. Right sides together, group the ivory and dark colored rectangles into pairs. Sew along one of the 2" edges.

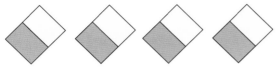

3. Piece the block.

❊ For each churn dash square, cut one ivory 2" square. Use the diagram below to guide the piecing of half-square triangles, connecting units and the middle square. Square up blocks to 5" square (cut size).

CONSTRUCTING THE QUILT

❊ Piece Churn Dash blocks and 72 plain squares into strips, using the diagram below as a guide. Since the blocks in this quilt are set "on point," notice how you piece diagonal rows rather than horizontal rows. When I pieced this quilt, I used full squares for the setting squares even at the edges of the quilt. I only cut the quilt's edges straight after the quilt was quilted.

❊ Sew these diagonal rows together. Before you trim the sides down to create the quilt top's finished rectangular shape, stay-stitch around the perimeter of the finished quilt about ¼" inside where the final cut line will be. This will help stabilize the bias edges that will be formed on the setting squares when you trim the quilt down to size. Note: Diagram below shows the quilt done in a different colorway.

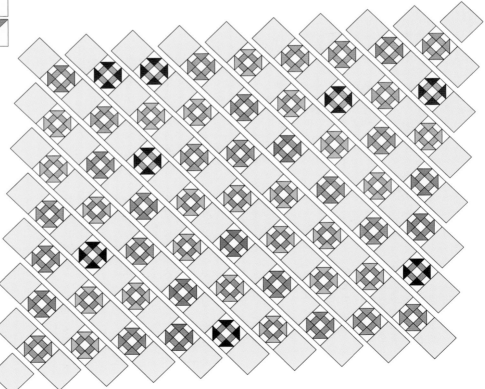

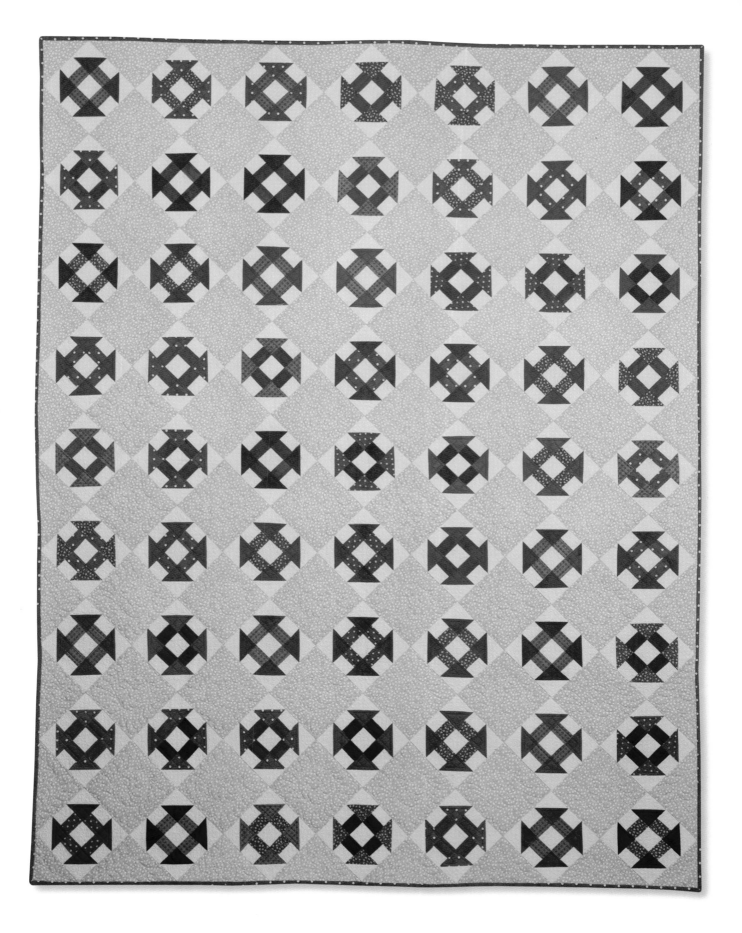

Strawberry Quilt

41" x 54" ✳ By Kim Gaddy

To make this sweet little quilt you will need to sew 28 strawberry blocks and 28 pinwheel blocks. Consult the chart on page 21 for block placement and border widths.

CUTTING GUIDE

For Strawberry Blocks:
Fabric for 84 green/ivory 1" finished-size half square triangles
- 112 – 1½" x 1½" squares, ivory fabric
- 56 – 2½" x 2½" squares, ivory fabric
- 56 – ¾" x 1½" rectangles, brown fabric
- 28 – 5½" x 5½" squares, strawberry fabric
- 42 – 2" squares green
- 42 – 2" squares ivory

For Pinwheel Blocks:
Fabric for 112 green/ivory 2" finished-size half square triangles
- 56 – 4½" x 1" ivory rectangles
- 56 – 5½" x 1½" ivory rectangles
- 56 – 3" squares green
- 56 – 3" squares ivory

For Sashing:
- 2 – 1½" x 37½" ivory rectangles
- 2 – 1½" x 48½" ivory rectangles

For Borders:
- 2 – 2½" x 50½" outer border rectangles
- 2 – 2½" x 41½" outer border rectangles

FABRIC
- 2 yards ivory
- ⅓ yard strawberry leaf green
- ⅛ yard strawberry stem brown
- ¾ yard strawberry red
- ½ yard pinwheel green
- ½ yard outer border fabric
- ½ yard for binding

STRAWBERRY BLOCKS

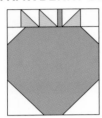

1. For each block sew three 1" finished size half-square triangles (HST). Use an ivory fabric and a green fabric. Use your favorite method to sew the half-square triangles or see page 23.

2. For each strawberry block, cut two 1½" ivory squares and one ¾" x 1½" brown rectangle for the stem. Piece the strawberry top together using the diagram as a guide.

3. Piece the strawberry.
For each strawberry block, cut the following:
- 1 – 5½" square of strawberry fabric
- 2 – 1½" squares of ivory fabric
- 2 – 2½" squares of ivory fabric

❋ Mark a diagonal line across the wrong side of each of the ivory squares.

❋ Using the diagram as a guide, place an ivory square at each corner of the strawberry square — small squares at the top, large squares at the bottom right sides together.

❋ Sew along the marked line, trim seam allowance and press seam towards the strawberry.

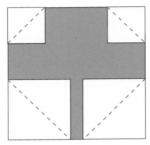

4. Sew the strawberry top to the strawberry. Note that the strawberry top is ½" longer than the strawberry. You can trim ¼" off each of the ivory squares before you sew the top to the bottom, or trim it after you sew the final seam as you trim up the strawberry block to its 5½" x 6½" cut size.

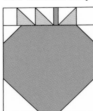

PINWHEEL BLOCK

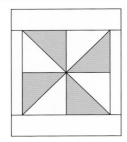

1. For each block sew four 2" finished size half-square triangles, using an ivory fabric and a green fabric. Use your favorite method to sew the half square triangles. I like to press the seams open.

2. Sew the half-square triangles together using the diagram as a guide.

  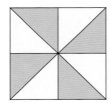

3. For the strawberry quilt, each pinwheel block has some extra sashing added to make the two blocks fit together.

❋ For each block you will need to cut two 4½" x 1" rectangles to add to the sides of each pinwheel block and two 5½" x 1½" rectangles to add to the top and bottom of the block. The block should measure 5½" x 6½".

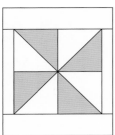

CONSTRUCTING THE QUILT

❋ Assemble the quilt following the diagram, alternating strawberry and pinwheel blocks. You'll have four rows with four strawberries and three pinwheel blocks and four rows with three strawberries and four pinwheel blocks. Attach borders.

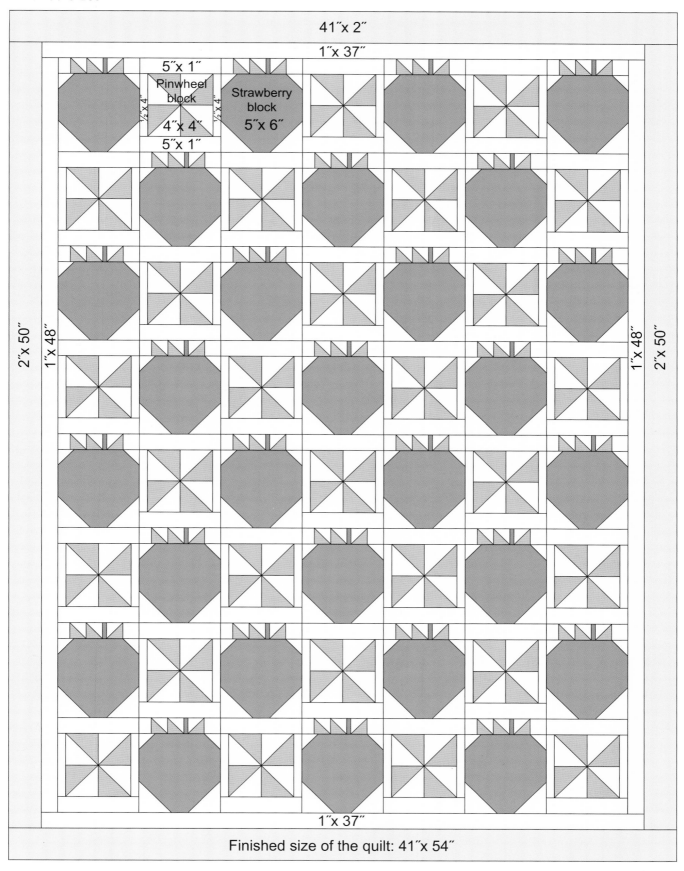

41″ x 2″

1″ x 37″

5″ x 1″

Pinwheel block

4″ x 4″

1/2″ x 4″

Strawberry block

5″ x 6″

1/2″ x 4″

5″ x 1″

2″ x 50″

1″ x 48″

1″ x 48″

2″ x 50″

1″ x 37″

Finished size of the quilt: 41″ x 54″

Hen and Chicks Quilt

37" x 37" ✳ By Kim Gaddy

CUTTING GUIDE

For Hen and Chicks Blocks:

- 144 – 1" finished yellow and ivory half-square triangles
- 288 – Template A ivory triangles
- 144 – Template B yellow triangles
- 144 – 1½" x 2½" ivory rectangles
- 36 – 1½" squares yellow (center square)
- 72 – 2" squares yellow
- 72 – 2" squares ivory

For Sashing:

- 84 – 1½" x 5½" ivory rectangles (sashing)
- 49 – 1½" x 1½" light green squares for setting squares

FABRIC

- 1 yard yellow, or 5 fat quarters for blocks
- ⅛ yard light green for setting squares
- 1¾ yard ivory for blocks and sashing
- ⅛ yard darker yellow for center square
- ⅜ yard for binding

HEN AND CHICKS BLOCKS

1. For each block sew four 1" finished size half-square triangles (HST). Use your favorite method to sew the half-square triangles. I often use preprinted foundation paper to sew these little guys, but I also like to use this method:

✳ Add 1" to the finished dimension of the half-square triangle to calculate the dimensions of squares to cut. In this case: 1" (finished size HST) + 1" (added seam allowance) = 2" square

✳ To make each Hen and Chick block, cut two 2" yellow squares and two 2" ivory squares. With a fabric pencil, mark a diagonal line across the wrong side of each ivory colored square. With right sides together, match each yellow square with an ivory square. Sew a seam ¼" away from each side of the marked line.

✳ Cut along the marked line. Press the seam towards the darker fabric. **Important:** These triangles are larger than needed. Trim each half-square triangle to 1½".

2. For each Hen & Chicks square, cut eight ivory triangles using Template A. Templates are on page 78. Right sides together, sew the shorter edge of the triangle to a yellow side of the half square triangle. To lessen fabric bulk at the yellow center point, press each seam towards the ivory triangles.

✳ Repeat for all half-square triangles.

3. Sew a yellow triangle (template B) to each side of the triangle unit completed in step number two.

✳ Cut four yellow triangles using template B. Sew a triangle to each triangle unit completed in step two. See the example below. The resulting square should measure 2½" unfinished.

✳ Press the seam towards the yellow triangle.

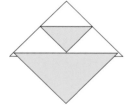

4. Complete the block. For each block cut four 1½" x 2½" ivory rectangles and one 1½" x 1½" yellow square.

CONSTRUCTING THE QUILT

✳ Use the diagram below as a guide for piecing. Where possible, press seams towards the yellow fabric.

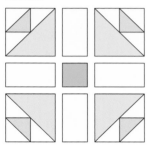

✳ Make 36 Hen and Chick blocks. Square up the blocks to 5½". Use the 1½" x 5½" ivory rectangles as sashing and the 1½" green squares as setting blocks to complete the quilt.

✳ I like to piece the individual rows. Some rows will be blocks and sashing, some rows will be sashing and setting squares. Lastly sew all the rows together. See diagram below.

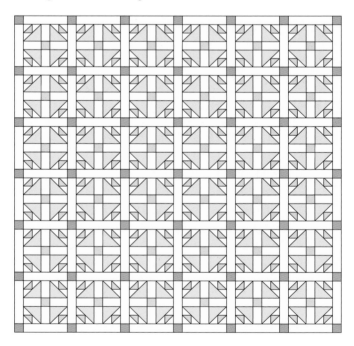

Basket Quilt

36" x 44" ✳ By Kim Gaddy

Sew 49 basket blocks and 50 nine patch blocks for this nice little lap quilt. Finished quilt measures 36" x 44". If you wish to make a simple 9-Patch quilt like the one on page 31, fabric amounts and cutting instructions are provided.*

CUTTING GUIDE
Basket Quilt
For Basket Blocks:
- 49 – 2½" x 4½" ivory rectangles
- 11 yards of ¼" brown bias tape
- 49 – Basket Block Template A pieces from brown
- 49 sets – Basket Template B pieces
(one each direction) from ivory

For 9-Patch Blocks:
- 250 – 1⅞" blue squares
- 200 – 1⅞" ivory squares

*Simple 9-Patch Quilt:
- 50 – 4½" squares
- 245 – 1⅞" bright print squares
- 196 – 1⅞" ivory print squares

9-PATCH BLOCK
✳ Done in blue and ivory, this little 9-Patch block makes the perfect spacer block for the Basket Quilt. Or, done in brights and a dominant print, this little block can stand alone.

✳ Note: The only thing tricky about this block is its size. In order to make this block fit with the 4" basket squares, I had to use somewhat irregular dimensions. Each finished-size square measures 1⅜".

FABRIC
Basket Quilt:
- 1⅛ yards brown for baskets
- 1½ yards ivory
- ¾ yard blue or five fat quarters
- ⅜ yard for binding

Simple 9-Patch Quilt:
- ⅔ yard ivory print
- 1 yard print for large squares
- Five fat quarters of assorted bright prints
- ⅜ yard for binding

1. Piece 9-patch square by square.

❋ For each 9-patch, cut five dark 1⅞" squares and four light ⅞" squares. Piece squares in a checkerboard pattern.

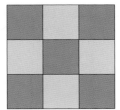

2. Or Piece 9-patch with strips:

❋ If you're making a bunch of 9-patch blocks as in this Basket quilt, then you may want to save some time by strip-piecing the blocks. To do this, cut four 1⅞" light colored strips (across the width of your fabric) for every five 1⅞" dark colored strips you cut. Piece strip units. You will need two dark-light-dark strip units for every one light-dark-light strip unit. See below.

❋ Press seams towards the dark fabric. Cut the strip units into 1⅞" rectangles. Use these rectangles to piece together the 9-patch blocks.

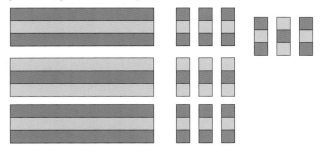

❋ **Note on 9-patches:** Trim each block down to 4½" square before piecing the quilt top.

BASKET BLOCK

1. Applique the basket handle. For each basket block, make an 8" long ¼" wide (finished) piece of bias tape out of the brown basket fabric. This will be the basket handle.

❋ Cut a 4½" x 2½" piece of ivory background fabric. Trace the basket handle onto the fabric with a fabric pencil.

❋ Applique the bias tape onto the background fabric to form the basket handle. I used fabric glue to hold the handle in place, then sewed it to the background fabric using my sewing machine's buttonhole stitch.

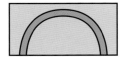

2. Piece the basket bottom. (Templates are on page 74.) For each basket, cut one basket template A piece out of brown and two basket template B pieces (one each direction) out of ivory fabric. Sew one template B piece to each side of the template A piece.

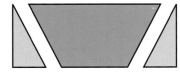

❋ Press seam towards basket.

3. Finish block. Sew handle unit to basket unit. Press seam towards the basket.

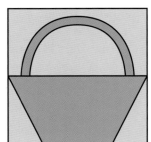

ASSEMBLY

✳ Make 11 rows of nine alternating 9-patch and basket blocks. Quilt and bind.

✳ To make an even faster quilt, replace basket blocks with solid blocks in a cute print.

Vegetable Quilt

40" x 40" ✳ By Kim Gaddy

This little quilt looks great draped over a sunroom chair, or hang it on your kitchen wall for a bit of summertime cheer in any season.

CUTTING GUIDE

✳ See vegetable dimensions on page 55 and templates on pages 76-78.

Cut:
- 9 onion blocks
- 11 turnip blocks
- 11 carrot blocks
- 10 tomato blocks
- 9 radish blocks

Also cut:
- 2 – 1" x 30½" rectangles, inner border
- 2 – 1" x 31½" rectangles, inner border
- 2 – 5½" x 31½" rectangles, outer border
- 2 – 5½" x 42½" rectangles, outer border

FABRIC
- ⅓ yard white, onion
- ⅛ yard purple, turnip
- ⅛ yard orange, carrot
- ⅛ yard red, tomato
- ⅛ yard pink, radish
- 1½ yards ivory or tan, background
- ⅙ yard dark gray, inner border
- ⅔ yard red dot, outer border
- Green scraps for stems
- ¾ yard for binding

CONSTRUCT THE QUILT

✳ Use the chart on page 34 and the individual block diagrams on pages 55 and 57 to piece the quilt center.

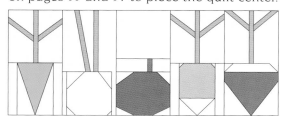

BORDER

❋ Add a ½" (finished size) inner border, then add a 5" (finished size) outer border. Mark, but do not cut, the scallop edge border. The diameter of the circle that forms each curve is 8¾".

QUILT

❋ As you bind the quilt, trim to the scallop edge. The border template is on page 75.

Finished Sizes

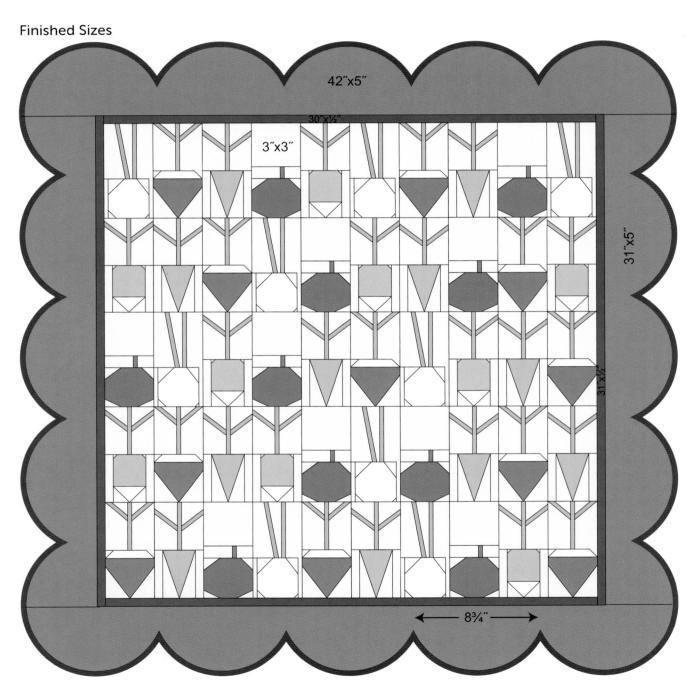

42"x5"

30"x½"

3"x3"

31"x5"

31"x½"

8¾"

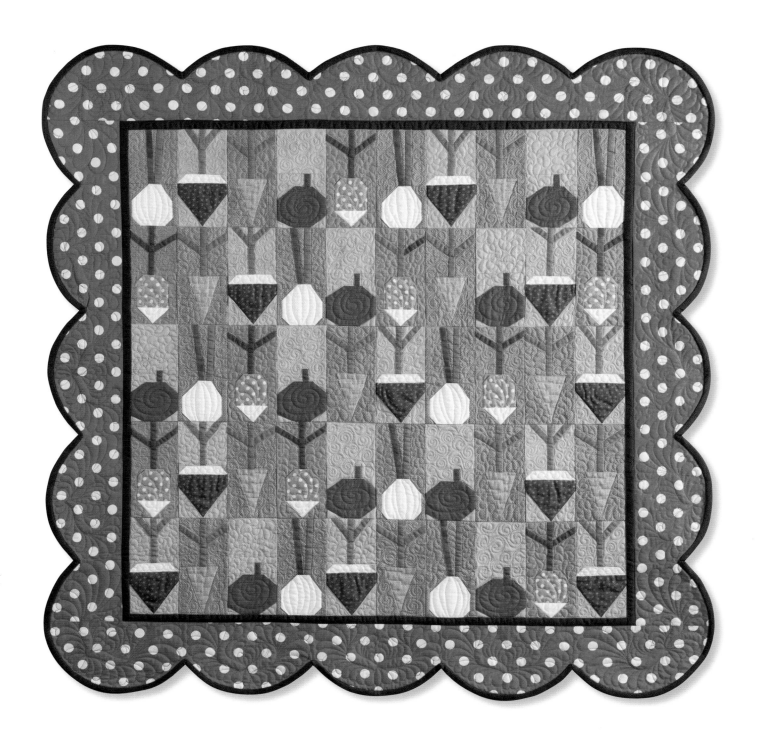

Bee Skep Table Topper

37" x 37" ❋ By Kim Gaddy

Ready for spring? This fabulous table topper is the perfect thing to brighten up your kitchen table.

CUTTING GUIDE
Templates are on page 74.
- 84 – 5½" x 1¼" strips, gold and brown
- 24 – 1½" x 1½" squares, ivory
- 12 – 5½" x 2½" rectangles, ivory
- 16 – 2" x 7¾" rectangles, ivory
- 4 – 8¼" x 8¼" squares, ivory
- 24 – 3½" x 3½" squares, ivory
- 25 – 3½" x 3½" squares, light yellow
- 4 – 21½" x 1" rectangles
- Light green strips to make about 3½ yards of ¼" bias tape for flower stems

CENTER
❋ Alternate ivory and yellow 3½" squares to piece the center checkerboard design. There are seven rows of seven squares. Note that there are four rows that begin and end with a yellow square and three rows that begin and end with a white square.

FABRIC
- Four ⅙ yard cuts from golds and browns
- 1¼ yards ivory
- ⅓ yard light yellow
- ¼ yard green (includes flower stem & leaves)
- ⅛ yard deep pink
- ⅛ yard or less of light pink
- ⅜ yard for binding

EXTRAS
- 12 – ¾" black buttons
- 4 – bee buttons

BEE SKEP BLOCK

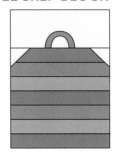

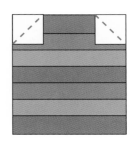

1. For each bee skep block, cut a 2½" x 5½" rectangle of ivory fabric. Using your favorite method, appliqué the bee skep handle to the rectangle.

2. Piece the bee skep.
   ※ Sew seven 1¼" x 5½" strips of gold and brown fabrics into a block that measures 5¾" x 5½". See the next diagram.

   ※ For each bee skep, cut two 1½" squares of ivory fabric.

   ※ Mark a diagonal line across the wrong side of each ivory square.

   ※ Using the diagram above as a guide, place an ivory square at each of the bee skep's top corners.

   ※ Sew along the marked lines, trim seam allowances and press the seams towards the bee skep.

3. Sew the handle block to the bee skep.

   ※ Trim the finished block to 5½" x 7¾".

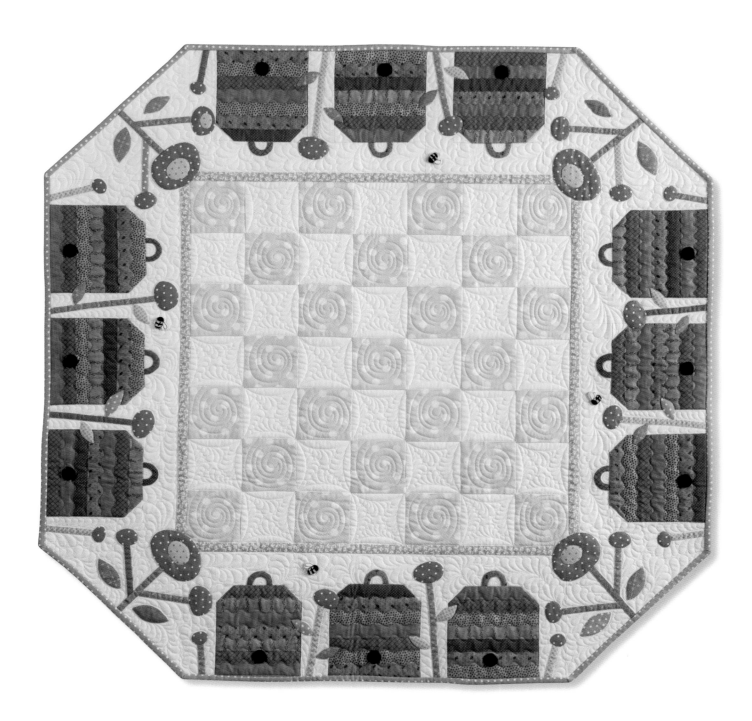

ASSEMBLY

✳ Piece four rows of three bee skeps. Join skeps with 2" x 7¾" ivory rectangles and add a rectangle to each side of the row. See diagram.

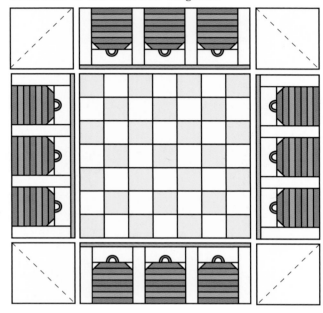

✳ Sew a green 1" strip to the top of the three-skep unit. Use the photo as a placement guide to add appliqued flowers.

✳ Sew the two bee skep units to the center checkerboard unit. Sew two 8¼" ivory squares to either side of two of the remaining two bee skep units, then sew them to either side of the checkerboard unit.

✳ To postpone having to work with un-sewn bias edges, leave the corner squares "square" until the quilt is quilted, then trim to the finished shape. Use a fabric marker to make a diagonal line across the four corner squares as in the diagram. Applique flowers on the corner piece. Cut on the marked line.

✳ Add bee buttons and ¾" black buttons for bee skep entries.

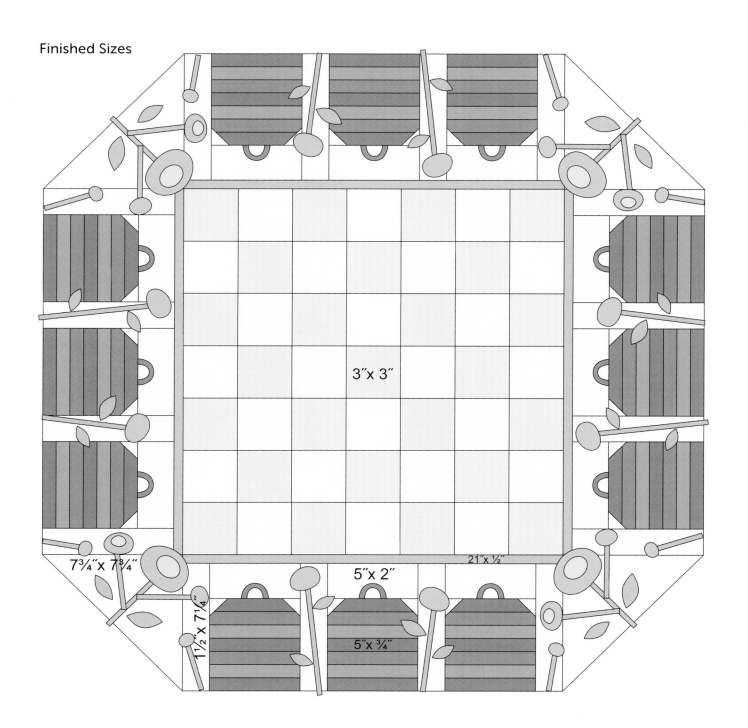

3″x 3″

21″x ½″

5″x 2″

7³⁄₄″x 7³⁄₄″

1½″ x 7¼″

5″x ¾″

Welcome Home Wallhanging

12" x 24" ✳ By Kim Gaddy

This is the perfect wallhanging for an entrance way or foyer. Even better, you can make it in one short afternoon. Use the diagram and instructions for the basket block, cherry block and lettering to complete the project.

CUTTING GUIDE

For the house:
Templates are on page 69.
- 2 – 3½" x 2½" ivory rectangles
- 2 – 2½" x 1½" ivory rectangles
- 1 – 6½" x 3½" ivory rectangle
- 2 – 2½" x 12½" ivory rectangles
- 2 – 1½" red squares
- 1 – 8½" x 12½" red rectangle
- 1 – 12½" x 1¾" green rectangle
- Blue bias tape for window sashing cut to fit windows
- Green bias tape for stems

For basket and cherry blocks:
Basket block is on page 74.
- 2 – 4½" x 4½" ivory squares
- 1 – 4½" x 2½" ivory rectangle
- 2 – basket block template B, ivory
- 1 – basket block template A, brown
- 8 – 2" x 2" blue squares
- 6 – ¾" buttons

For connecting pieces:
- 1 – 12½" x 1¼" gray rectangle
- 1 – 12½" x 2" gray rectangle
- 1 – 12½" x 4" ivory rectangle

FABRIC
- ½ yard ivory
- ¼ yard red
- ⅛ yard green
- Scraps of violet, yellow, blue, black, brown and gray
- Approximately 6" x 10" felted wool for the lettering
- ¾ yard ¼" wide green single fold bias tape for flower stems
- ¾ yard ³⁄₁₆" wide blue single fold bias tape for window sashing
- Scrap of brown for ¼" wide bias tape for basket handle
- ⅓ yard for binding

EXTRA
- Buttons for flower centers and doorknob
- Buttons for cherries, star button for basket and heart button for Welcome panel

CHERRY BLOCK

1. Cut the fabric for the two blocks.

2. Piece the block.
* Mark a diagonal line across the wrong side of each of the blue squares. Place a blue square at each corner of the ivory square right sides together. Sew along the marked lines, trim seam allowances and press seams towards corners.

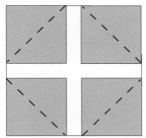

3. Appliqué the leaves. Templates are on page 69.
* Using the diagram as a guide, appliqué the cherry leaves.

* **Note:** On one project my quilter "quilted in" the cherry stems, on another project, I embroidered the cherry stems. Buttons will be added after quilting.

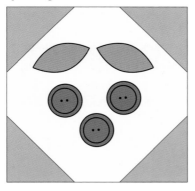

HOUSE BLOCK

1. Piece the house. Templates are on page 69.
* Using the diagram as a placement guide (note: dimensions on the guide are finished dimensions), piece together the house block.

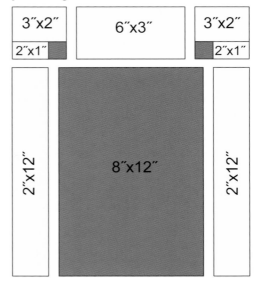

2. Appliqué the details.
* Using the diagram as a guide, appliqué the door, windows, and roof and bird. Next add bias tape details—window divisions and flower stems. Appliqué flowers, leaves and bird too. Bird template is on page 73.

3. Finish the block.

❊ Sew the "grassy" bottom rectangle to the house block.

12"x1¼"

❊ Appliqué the wool lettering to the 12½" x 4" ivory rectangle. See instructions on page 7. Sew completed rectangle to the bottom of the house unit.

❊ Add the 12½" x 2" gray strip to the bottom of the unit and the 12½" x 1¼" strip to the top of the unit.

❊ Sew one basket block (see page 74) and two cherry blocks. Piece together. Sew to the top of the house unit.

❊ Quilt and bind.

❊ Add 3 – ¾" buttons for cherries and add buttons to flowers and Welcome strip.

❊ This wallhanging is narrow enough that you can simply tack a small plastic cafe rod ring to each corner to use as a hanging device.

Finished Sizes

12″x ¾″

12″x 3½″

Welcome

12″x1½″

Afternoon Walk Pillow

22" x 12" ❊ By Kim Gaddy

Here's a great pillow for the backyard poultry enthusiast in your life. This pillow will fit a 12" x 22" pillow form.

CUTTING GUIDE

❊ See chicken and chick block instructions for individual block cutting dimensions. Flower and leaf templates are on page 74.
You will also need:

- 1 – 6½" x 4" rectangle, ivory
- 1 – 17½" x 2" rectangle, green
- 2 – dark brown 17½" x 1" strips
- 2 – 9" x 1" dark brown strips
- 2 – 17½" x 2½" rectangles, border fabric
- 2 – 3" x 12½" rectangles, border fabric
- 1 – 22½" x 12½" rectangle, pillow back

FABRIC

- ¼ yard ivory
- ¼ yard border
- ⅛ yard dark brown
- ⅛ yard green
- ⅜ yard pillow backing
- Scraps of orange, yellow, green, blue, violet and four browns
- Wool felt for chick legs/beak and hen combs
- 2 yards wide rickrack
- Small buttons for hen's eyes and flower centers
- One 12" x 22" pillow form

CHICKEN BLOCK

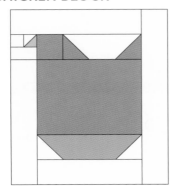

1. For each chicken or rooster cut the following pieces:
   - 3 – 1½" squares, chicken body fabric
   - 1 – 4½" x 3" rectangle, chicken body fabric
   - 1 – 4½" x 1½" rectangle, lighter chicken fabric
   - 2 – 1½" squares, ivory
   - 1 – 1" square, orange
   - 2 – 1" squares, ivory
   - 1 – 1½" x 1" rectangle, ivory
   - 2 – 1½" x 5½" rectangles, ivory
   - 1 – 4½" x 1½" rectangle, ivory
   - 1 – 3½" x 1½" rectangle, ivory
   - 1 – 1½" x 7½" rectangle, ivory (optional)

2. Piece the chicken.
   ✳ Mark a diagonal line across the wrong side of two of the 1½" chicken body squares.

   ✳ Using the diagram as a guide, place a brown square on either side of the 3½" x 1½" ivory rectangle. Sew along the marked lines, trim seam allowances and press seams towards the brown fabric.

   ✳ Sew the third 1½" square of brown fabric to the left side of the above unit.

✳ Sew the 4½" x 3½" rectangle to the bottom of this piece.

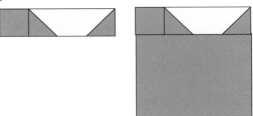

✳ Mark a diagonal line across the wrong side of the two 1½" ivory squares.

✳ Using the diagram as a guide, place an ivory square on either side of the 4½" x 1½" lighter brown chicken fabric. Sew along the marked lines, trim seam allowances and press seams towards the brown fabric. See below.

✳ Sew this unit to the bottom of the chicken body proper.

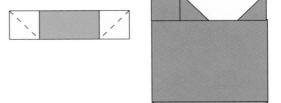

3. Sew the beak.
   ✳ Mark a diagonal line across the wrong side of one 1" ivory square. Right sides together, place the ivory square on top of the 1" orange square. Sew along the marked line. Trim the seam. Press the seam open. You should have a ½" finished size half square triangle. Sew the other 1" ivory square to the left side of this unit, and then sew the 1½" x 1" ivory rectangle to the bottom of the beak unit.

4. Add background pieces.

❋ Sew the 4½" x 1½" ivory rectangle to the bottom of the chicken unit and the 1½" x 5½" ivory rectangle to the bottom of the beak unit.

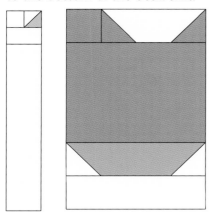

❋ Next, sew the 5½" x 1½" ivory rectangle to the top of the chicken unit. Depending on how you are using the chicken blocks, you may wish to sew a 1½" x 7½" ivory rectangle to the right side of the chicken unit. If you are making the block for the sampler quilt or pillow only one of the chickens has this final spacer block.

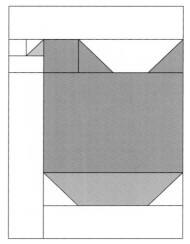

5. Appliqué details.

❋ Cut ⅛" strips from felted wool or felt for the hen's legs. Use the pattern template to cut the hen's combs from the wool or felt. Machine or hand stitch in place. See quilt photo for placement.

Comb template

Waddle

CHICK BLOCK

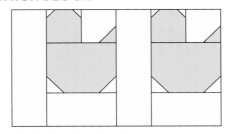

1. For each chick block cut the following pieces:
   - 1 – 1½" square, yellow
   - 1 – 1" square, yellow
   - 1 – 2½" x 2" rectangle, yellow
   - 2 – ¾" squares, ivory
   - 2 – 1" squares, ivory
   - 1 – 1½" square, ivory
   - 1 – 2½ x 1½" rectangle, ivory
   - 1 – or 2 – 1½" x 4" rectangles, ivory

2. Piece chick.
   ❋ Mark a diagonal line across the wrong side of two of the ¾" ivory squares. Using the diagram to the top as a guide, place an ivory square on each top corner of the 1½" yellow square. Sew along the marked lines, trim seam allowances and press seams open. This is the chick's head.

   ❋ Mark a diagonal line across the wrong side of the 1" yellow square. Using the diagram below as a guide, place the yellow square on the bottom right corner of the 1½" ivory square. Sew on the drawn lines, trim away the seam allowances and press toward the yellow. Sew this "tail" unit to the right of the chick "head" unit.

 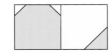

❋ Mark a diagonal line across the wrong side of the two 1" ivory squares. Using the diagram below as a guide, place an ivory square on either lower corner of the 2½" x 2" yellow rectangle. Sew along the marked lines, trim seam allowances and press seams open. This is the chick body.

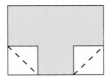

❋ Sew chick head and tail unit to the top of the chick body unit. Sew a 2½" x 1½" ivory rectangle to the bottom of the chick unit. Sew a 1½" x 4" ivory rectangle to the left side of the chick block. Depending on how you are using your chick block, you may wish to add another rectangle to the right side of the chick.

3. Appliqué details.
   ❋ Cut ⅛" strips from felted wool or felt for the chick's legs. Use the pattern template to cut the chick's beak from the wool or felt. Machine or hand stitch in place. See pillow photo on page 48 for placement.

DIRECTIONS

✳ Use the diagram below to piece the pillow top. Sew the 17½" x 2" green strip to the bottom of the hen and chick unit. Press seam towards the green fabric. Before adding borders, add the appliqué and button details. See pillow photo for placement ideas.

✳ Sew a 17½" x 2¼" strip to the top and bottom of the hen and chick unit, then sew a 3" x 12½" strip to the right and left sides of the unit. Right sides together, sew the pillow back to the pillow top leaving a hole for turning and stuffing. Add rickrack trim in the seam if desired. Turn the pillow and stuff or use a purchased pillow form. Whip stitch the opening closed.

✳ Optional inner trim: Cut two 17½" x 1" and two 9" x 1" strips from dark brown fabric. Fold each strip in half, down the long edge, wrong sides together, to make four narrow pieces of trim. Baste these strips around the edges of the pillow center with the folded edges of the brown strips facing the inside of the pillow center—shorter strips matching the short sides of the pillow and long strips with the long sides.

Finished Sizes

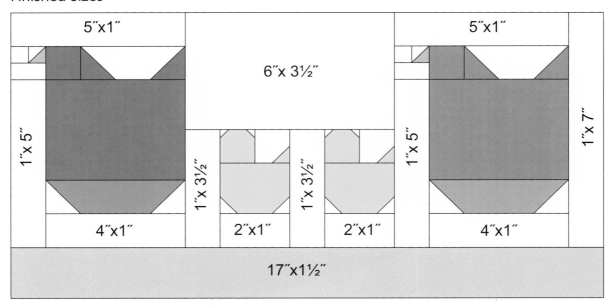

Vegetable Runner

18" x 41" ✳ By Kim Gaddy

This cheery table runner will brighten any table. Use the dimensions below (finished dimensions) to piece the top.

VEGGIE BLOCKS

1. Cut the fabric for two of each of the five vegetables.

✳ Use the diagrams below and the templates on page 76-78 to cut fabric for each vegetable block. Note that dimensions are finished dimensions. Add ½" to each measurement to obtain cutting dimensions.

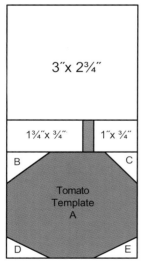

3"x 2¾"

1¾"x ¾"   1"x ¾"

B   C
Tomato Template A
D   E

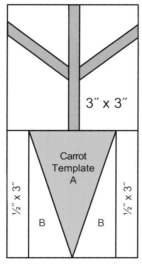

3" x 3"

Carrot Template A

½" x 3"   ½" x 3"

B   B

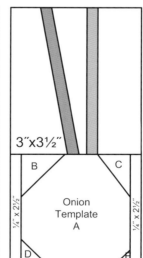

3"x3½"

B   C
Onion Template A
D   E

¼" x 2½"   ¼" x 2½"

FABRIC

- ⅛ yard green
- ⅛ yard yellow
- ⅔ yard center fabric (bias check)
- ⅔ yard background fabric (black)
- Scraps of white, orange, red, purple, pink, brown and light green
- ⅓ yard for binding

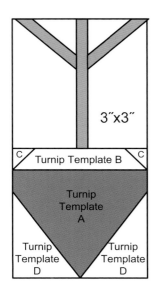

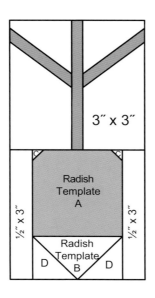

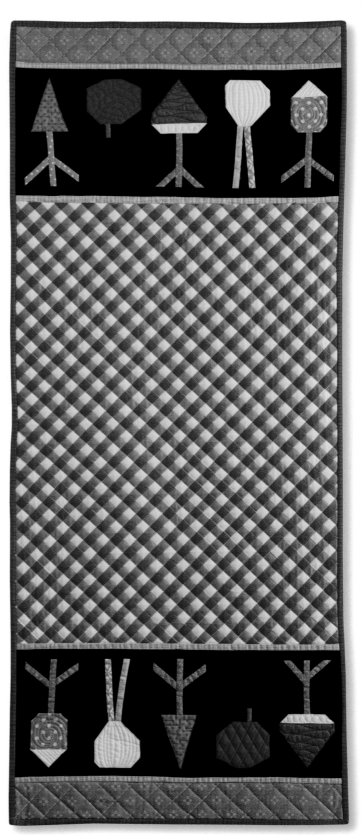

✻ Make single fold ¼" bias tape for the stems, except for the tomato. The tomato stem is a ¼" x ¾" (finished dimension) piece or fabric that is pieced into the background.

2. Applique the stem.

✻ Using the diagram to the right as a placement guide, appliqué the stems onto the background fabric.

3. Piece the blocks.

✻ Using the diagrams as a guide, piece each vegetable block. Sew each of the two rows of vegetables together, joining blocks with sashing strips. Attach gold and green strips to the top and bottom of the vegetable rows and then attach these to either end of the runner's center.

Finished Sizes

Give Thanks Runner

19" x 47" ❋ By Kim Gaddy

This simple table runner is fabulous for the fall holidays or any days. See page 7 for instructions on appliquéing the lettering.

CUTTING GUIDE

Bird template is on page 73.

- 6 green 2" squares
- 6 ivory 2" squares
- 24 – 1½" squares, ivory fabric for the pumpkin blocks
- 12 – 1½" x 2½" rectangles, ivory fabric for pumpkin top
- 6 – 5½" x 1½" ivory rectangles for top of pumpkin block
- 8 – 1½" x 6½" ivory rectangles for sashing pumpkins
- 2 – 6½" x 19½" ivory rectangles for Give Thanks background
- 6 – ¾" x 1½" rectangles, brown fabric for the pumpkin stems
- 6 – 5½" x 4½" rectangles, orange fabric for the pumpkins
- 4 – 1¾" x 19½" grey strips
- 2 – 3½" x 19½" rectangles, medium green for the borders
- 1 – 9½" x 19½" rectangles, medium green for the center
- 2 – 2¼" x 19½" light green strips

FABRIC

- ½ yard ivory
- ⅛ yard light green
- ⅓ yard medium green
- ⅛ yard gray
- Scraps of brown for stems
- ⅙ yard orange
- 6" x 10" felted wool for lettering
- ⅓ yard for binding

PUMPKIN BLOCK

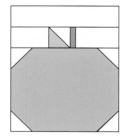

1. For each block sew one ivory and green 1½" half-square triangle. Use your favorite method to sew the half-square triangles or see page 23 for directions.

2. Piece pumpkin top.

❋ For each pumpkin block, use two 1½" x 2½" ivory rectangles and one ¾" x 1½" brown rectangle for the stem. Sew the pumpkin top together using the diagram as a guide.

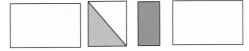

3. Piece the pumpkin: For each pumpkin block, mark a diagonal line across the wrong side of each of the 1½" ivory squares.

❋ Using the diagram as a guide, place an ivory square at each corner of an orange rectangle. Sew along the marked lines, trim seam allowances and press seams toward the pumpkin.

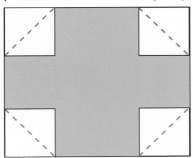

4. Sew the pumpkin top to the pumpkin: **Note that the pumpkin top is longer than the pumpkin.** You can trim to size the left-most ivory rectangle before you sew the top to the bottom, or trim it afterwards.

❋ For each pumpkin block cut a 5½" x 1½" ivory rectangle. Sew this to the top of each pumpkin unit. Trim the finished pumpkin block to its 5½" x 6½".

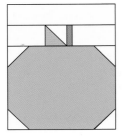

DIRECTIONS

❋ Sew six pumpkin blocks. Piece them in two rows of three using 1½" x 6½" connecting strips. Note that there is a connecting strip on each end of the pumpkin rows.

❋ Use the diagram for placement to applique the crow to the pumpkin unit.

❋ Use instructions on page 7 to applique the "Give Thanks" wool lettering on two 6½" x 19½" ivory rectangles. Template is on page 82.

❋ Sew pumpkin units, wool lettering units, and green and gray strips together using the diagram as a placement guide.

❋ Quilt and bind.

Finished Sizes

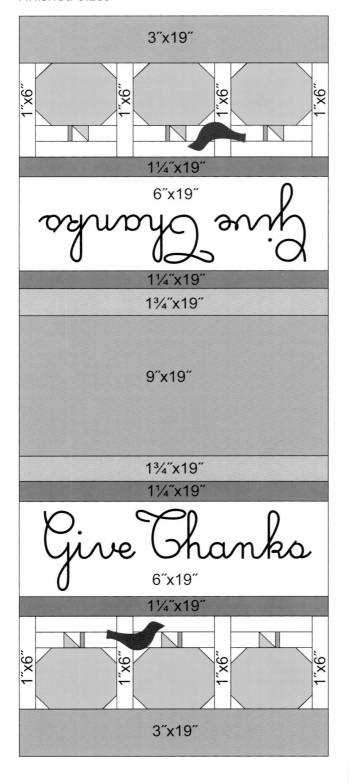

3"x19"

1"x6"   1"x6"   1"x6"   1"x6"

1¼"x19"

6"x19"

Give Thanks

1¼"x19"

1¾"x19"

9"x19"

1¾"x19"

1¼"x19"

Give Thanks

6"x19"

1¼"x19"

1"x6"   1"x6"   1"x6"   1"x6"

3"x19"

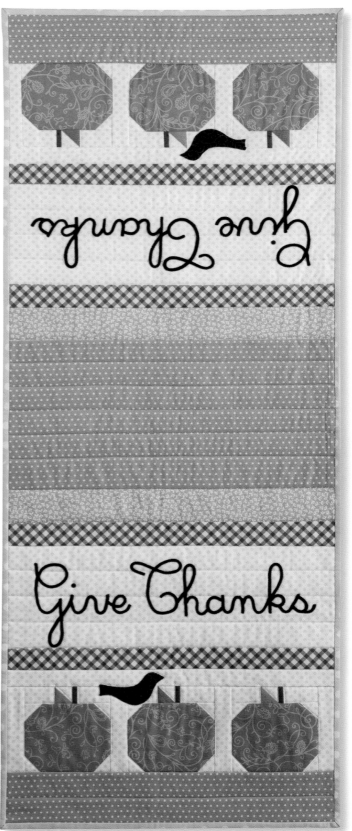

Vegetable Mat

15" x 18" ✳ By Kim Gaddy ✳ Embroidery by Connie McKay

CUTTING

✳ Templates are on pages 70-73. Trace the vegetable shapes onto the paper side of freezer paper with a fine tip permanent marker. Cut out the shapes directly on the lines. Iron the wax side of the paper shapes to the wool. Cut out the shapes. Remove paper. Note: Some shapes are easier to free-hand cut.

✳ Use the freezer paper method to cut front and back penny pieces from black wool. Likewise, cut the center oval and lining pieces.

BASTE THE WOOL SHAPES

✳ Lay the wool design pieces out on the black circles. Baste in place. I use a fabric glue like Roxanne's Glue Baste It.

SEW THE DESIGN

✳ Using two strands of matching embroidery floss, buttonhole stitch or whipstitch the pattern pieces to the background fabric. After all the pieces are sewn in place, add embroidered details like French Knots and stem stitching.

✳ Sew penny backing to the penny top: Place a wool backing piece on the back of each appliquéd penny. Using two strands of floss, buttonhole stitch around the edge of each penny. Place the completed pennies around the center oval. Sometimes the pennies "shrink" as they are appliquéd and sewn and the center oval may need to be cut down slightly. Make adjustments as needed, and then attach the lining to the center oval piece.

✳ Using two strands of black embroidery floss, tack the pennies to the center oval and to each other. I take about three tacking stitches to secure each penny. The black floss will disappear in the wool.

SUPPLIES

- 1 fat quarter of black wool
- 1 fat quarter of backing wool
- Scraps of wool, none larger than 3" squares: purple, light purple, white, pink, brown, pumpkin orange, carrot orange, lemon yellow, apple red, strawberry, cherry red, tomato red, pear green, bright green, kelly green, light, medium and dark leaf green
- Embroidery floss in colors that match wool
- Fabric glue

Farm Animal Tea Towels

By Kim Gaddy

CUTTING GUIDE

For each towel:

- 1 – tea towel (or cut osnaburg or another soft woven fabric to your preferred size)
- 1 – 2" wide strip of fabric the same length as the tea towel's width plus ½" for seam allowance
- 1 – 6½" wide strip of fabric the same length as the tea towel's width plus ½" for seam allowance. (If you want to make the towel end ruffled, cut this piece about 42" long or from seam allowance to seam allowance.)

DIRECTIONS

(See appliqué notes on page 66.)

❉ Appliqué the animal shape to the middle of the towel about 1½" to 2" from the bottom edge. If using a pre-sewn tea towel, cut off the hemmed edge to lessen bulk when adding bottom trim.

❉ Right sides together, fold the 2" wide piece of trim along the long edge. Sew along the 1" wide edges. Trim the corner, turn inside out and press the long fold.

❉ Right sides together, fold the 6½" wide piece of trim along the long edge. Sew along the 3¼" wide edges. Trim corner, turn and press the long fold.

❉ At the appliquéd edge of the tea towel, lay the narrower trim on the right side of the tea towel, and then add the wider piece of trim on top of that. Pin in place. Sew with a ¼" seam allowance. Zigzag or serge the raw edge.

❉ Press the narrower piece of trim towards the towel body. Using matching thread, sew along the folded edge to attach to the towel.

FABRIC

For each towel:

- 1 towel or osnaburg or other soft woven fabric
- ½ yard ivory
- ¼ yard red
- ⅛ yard green
- Scraps of violet, yellow, blue, black, brown and gray
- Felted wool for the lettering

FARM ANIMAL APPLIQUÉ PIECES

❋ I use a variety of appliqué techniques when I sew. When I want to appliqué an item that will be exposed to a lot of wear and tear, I like to use fusible webbing and finish the edges with a tight zigzag stitch. Other times, I use a very traditional needle-turn method. When I want the look of traditional needle turn but with a little more durability (and I don't have a lot of time to sew) I compromise and use this "fake" needle-turn method. Here's how I do it:

❋ Trace the appliqué shapes on to the paper side of freezer paper. (Note: Trace the mirror image of shapes that are not symmetrical or else they will face the opposite direction when finished.)

❋ Cut the shapes out on the lines.

❋ Iron the wax side of the freezer paper shapes to the wrong side of the fabric.

❋ Cut out shapes leaving about ⅛ inch between the paper shape and the cutting line.

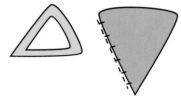

❋ Leave the wax paper on the shape. With a 'wand' type iron, iron the raw edges of the fabric towards the paper. Clip inward curves only — and then only where absolutely necessary.

❋ Remove the paper and glue the raw edges down with a little bit of fabric glue. I like Roxanne's Glue Baste It because it has a fine-tip applicator.

❋ Arrange appliqué shapes on the background fabric and glue baste in place.

❋ Set up your sewing machine. Put thread in the bobbin that matches the color of appliqué shape you are going to sew. If your bobbin has a little hole on the bobbin case that you can 'thread' your bobbin thread through to give you a little more bobbin tension, do so.

❋ Thread the top spool with invisible thread. My favorite thread for this is YLI brand invisible thread. There is a 'light' invisible for light colored fabrics and a 'smoky' colored invisible that is great for darker fabrics.

❋ Put a "wide" foot on your sewing machine. Try the foot you use to zigzag stitch. You will want to be able to see where your needle is going when you appliqué.

❋ Set the stitch on your machine to either a blind hem stitch or a buttonhole stitch. You will have to experiment with stitches and stitch settings for this part. You are looking for a couple of running stitches (to go along the side of the appliqué shape) and then a small "stitch in" that will catch a bit of the appliqué shape's fabric. Once you find a stitch setting that works, practice on some scrap appliqué. It won't take long to get the hang of it.

❋ I also like to set my machine to a 'needle down' setting so that I can turn corners easily. If you have a bar that you can use to raise and lower the presser foot with your leg, that will also help you speed up sewing around curves.

❋ Note: When you sew, the stitches should lie tightly next to the appliqué shape. In the diagram, they are spaced farther away for demonstration purposes.

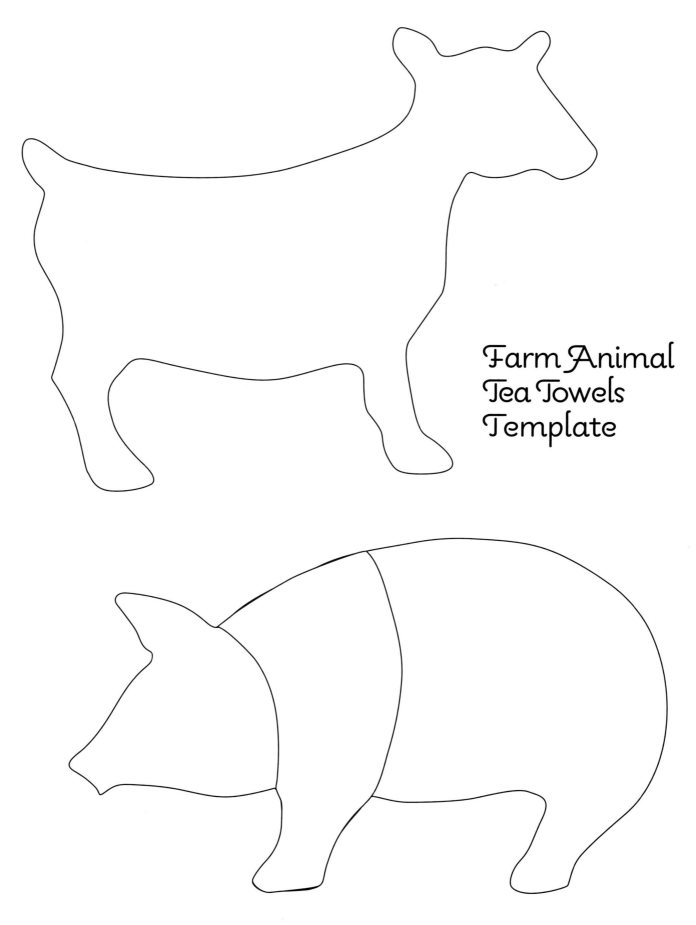

Farm Animal
Tea Towels
Template

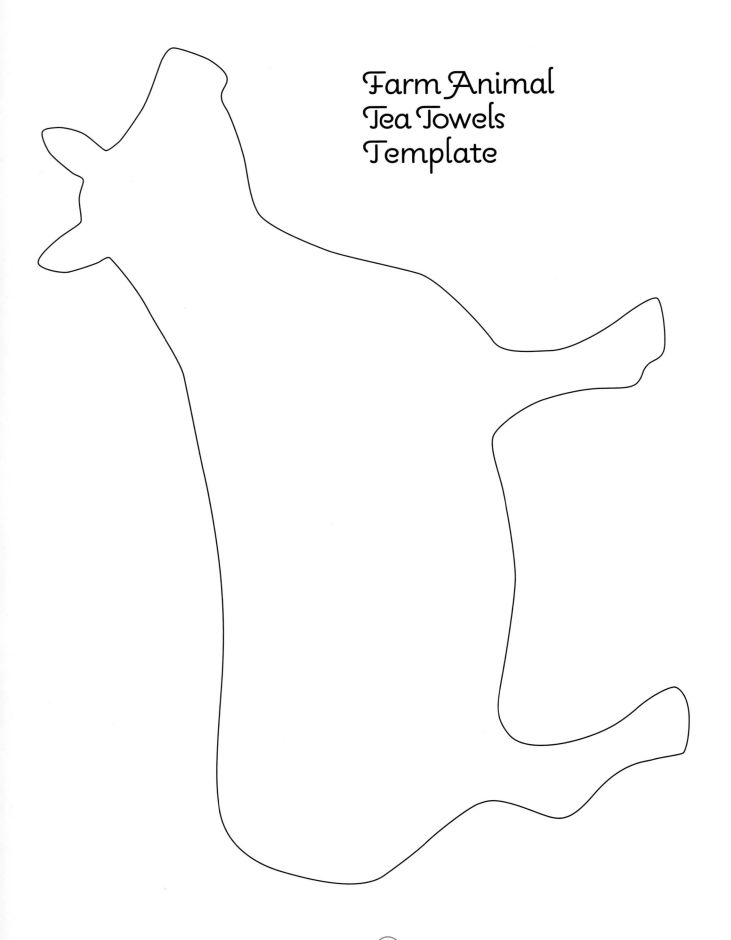

Farm Animal
Tea Towels
Template

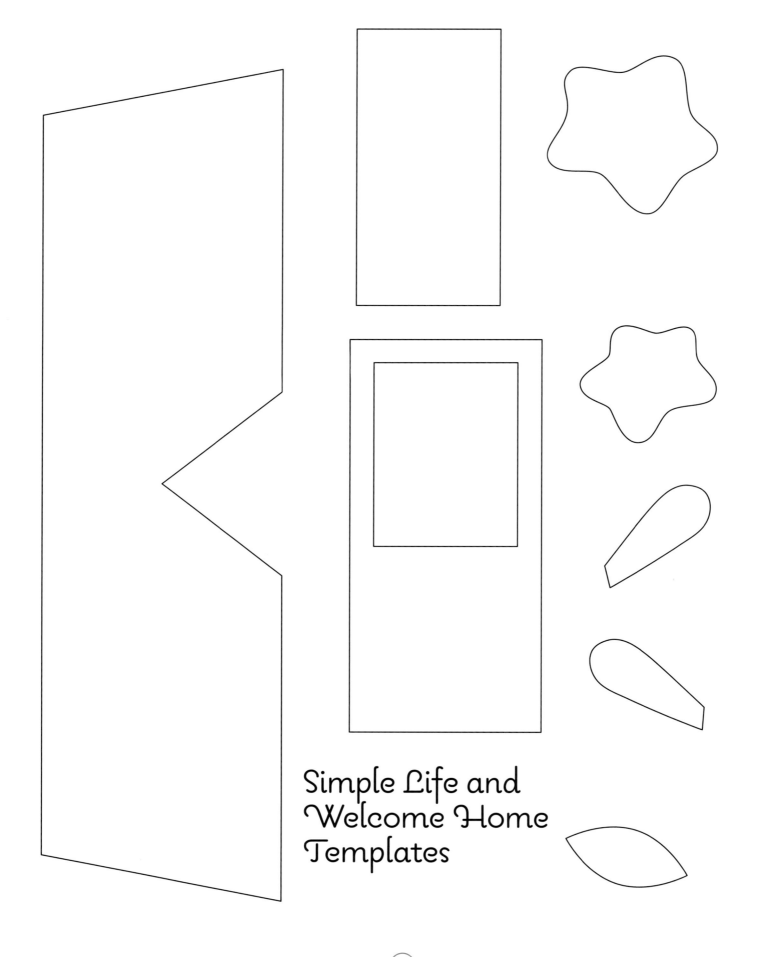

Simple Life and
Welcome Home
Templates

Vegetable Mat Templates

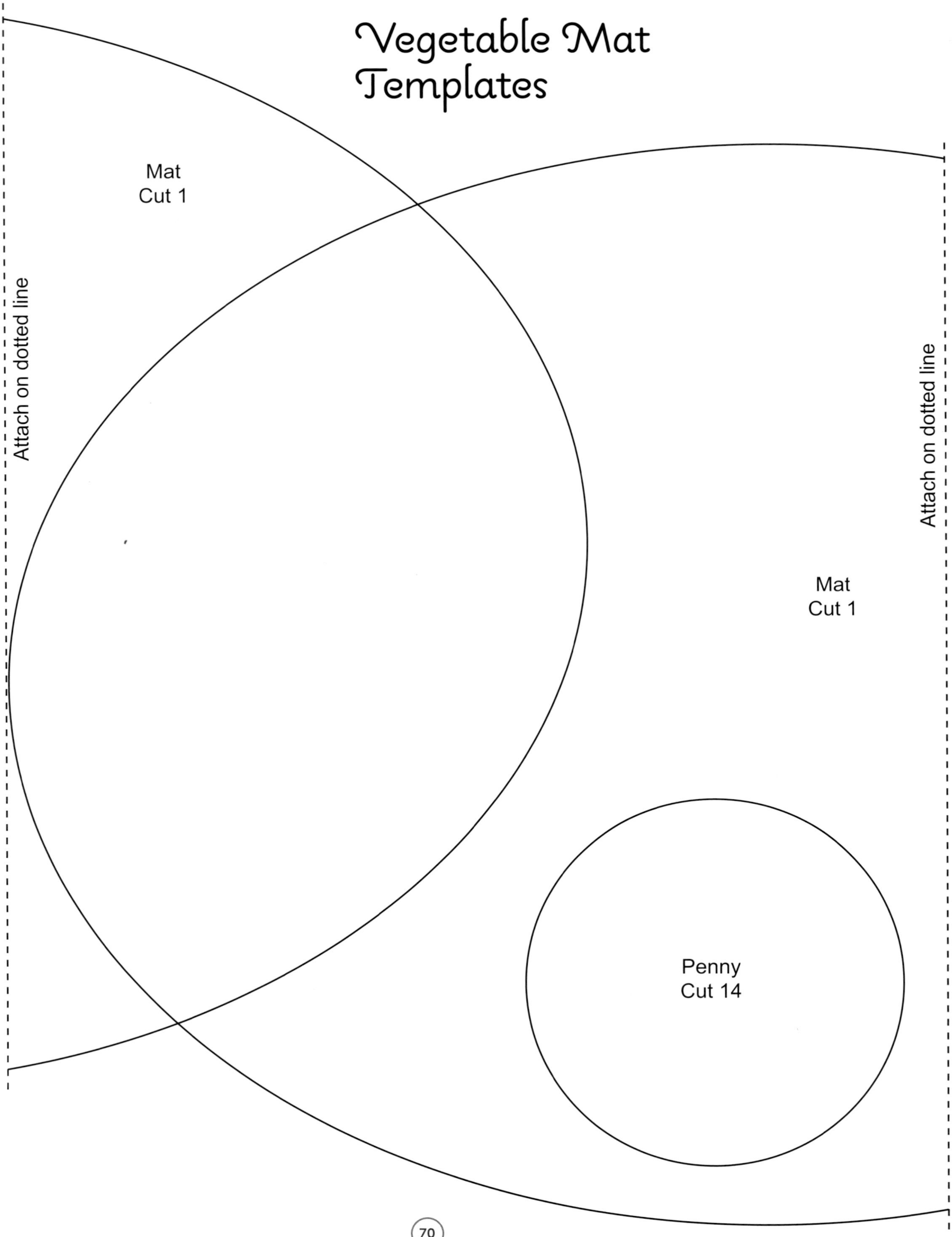

Mat
Cut 1

Mat
Cut 1

Penny
Cut 14

Vegetable Mat Templates

Vegetable Mat Templates

Bird template for
Give Thanks Runner and
Welcome Home Wallhanging

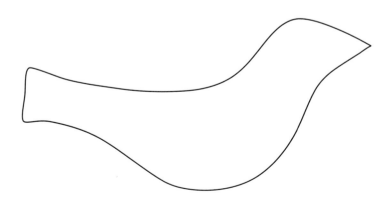

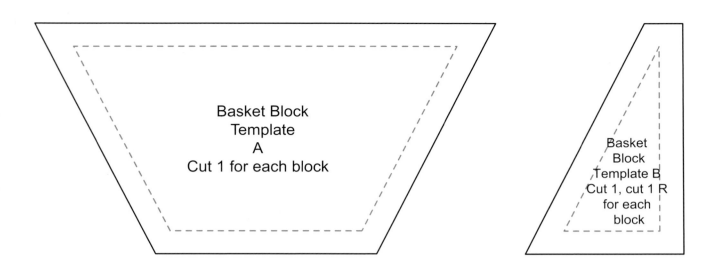

Basket Block
Template
A
Cut 1 for each block

Basket
Block
Template B
Cut 1, cut 1 R
for each
block

Basket Quilt
Templates

Bee Skep Table Topper Templates
and Afternoon Walk
flower and leaf templates

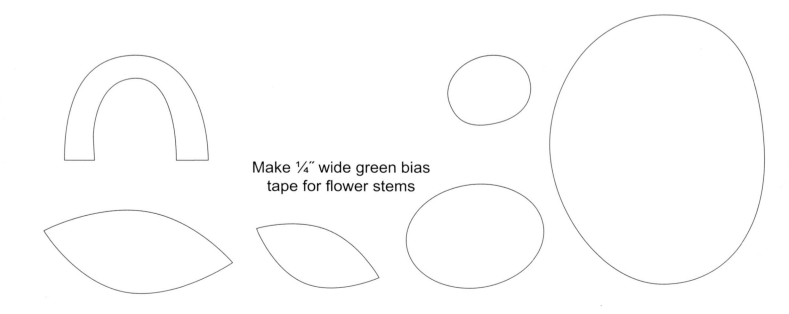

Make ¼″ wide green bias
tape for flower stems

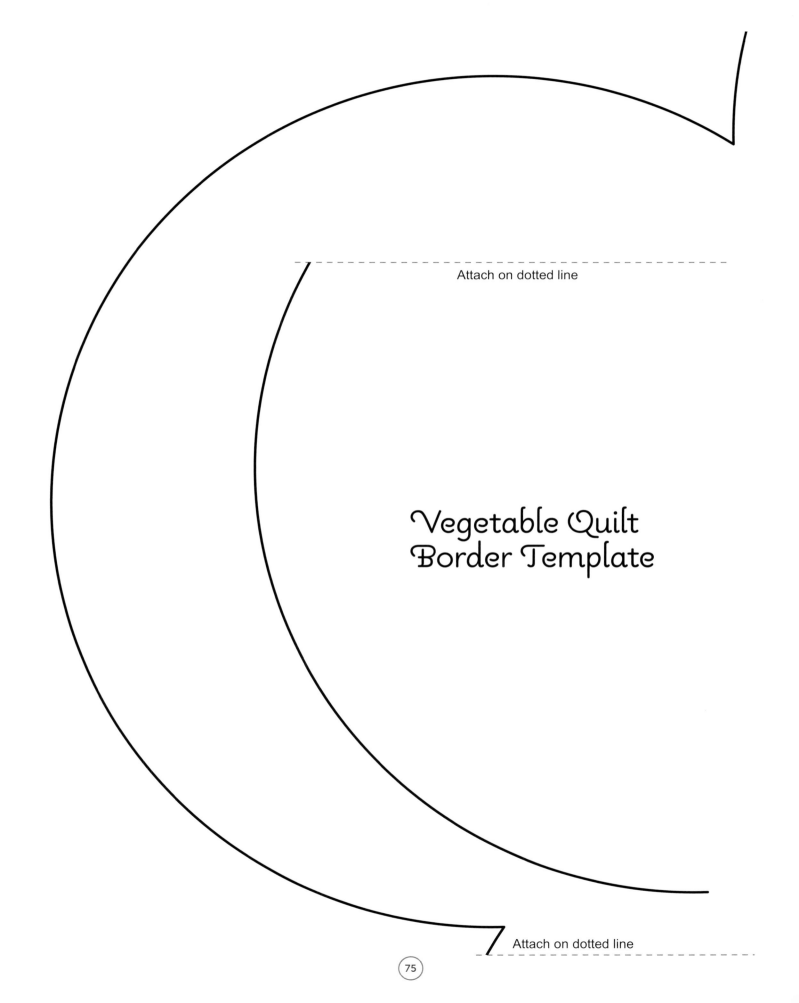

Attach on dotted line

Vegetable Quilt
Border Template

Attach on dotted line

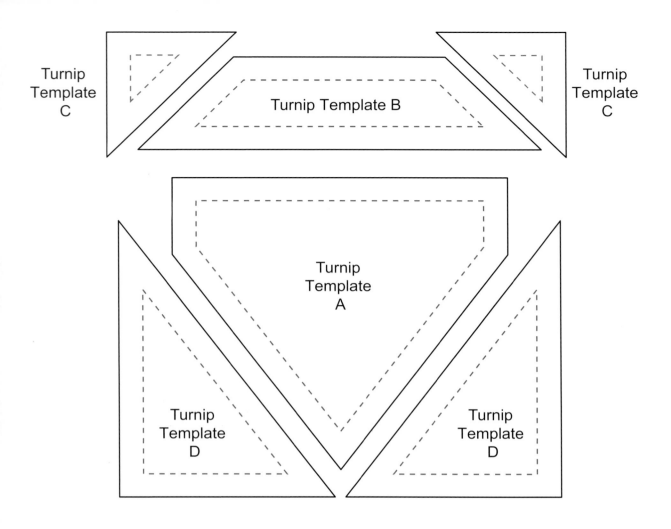

Turnip
Template
C

Turnip Template B

Turnip
Template
C

Turnip
Template
A

Turnip
Template
D

Turnip
Template
D

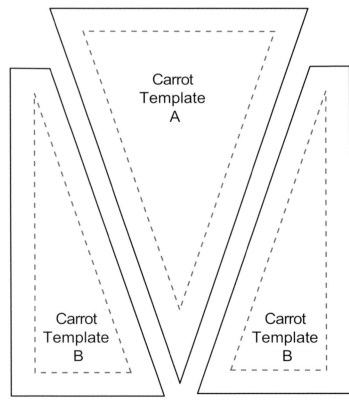

Carrot
Template
A

Carrot
Template
B

Carrot
Template
B

Vegetable Quilt
& Runner
Templates

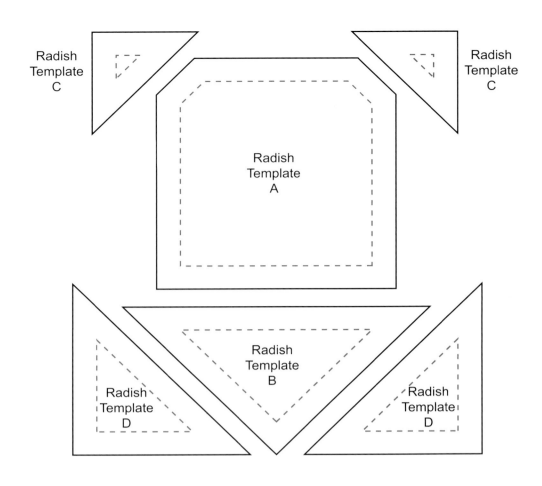

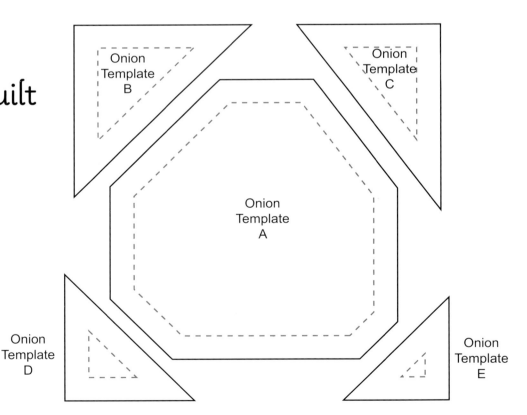

Vegetable Quilt
& Runner
Templates

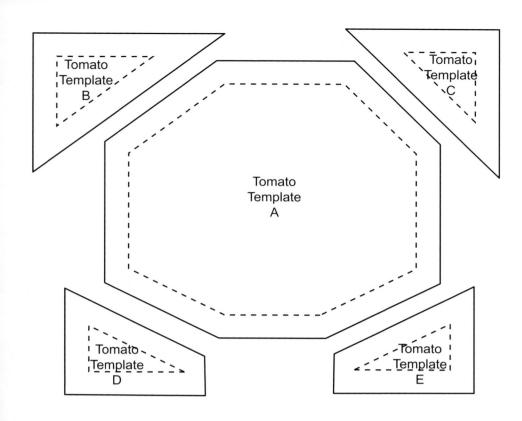

Tomato
Template
B

Tomato
Template
C

Tomato
Template
A

Tomato
Template
D

Tomato
Template
E

Vegetable Quilt & Runner Templates

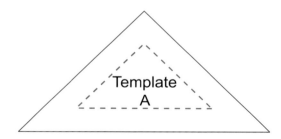

Template
A

Hen and Chicks Templates

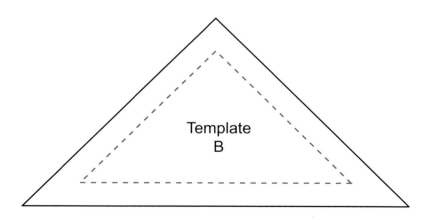

Template
B

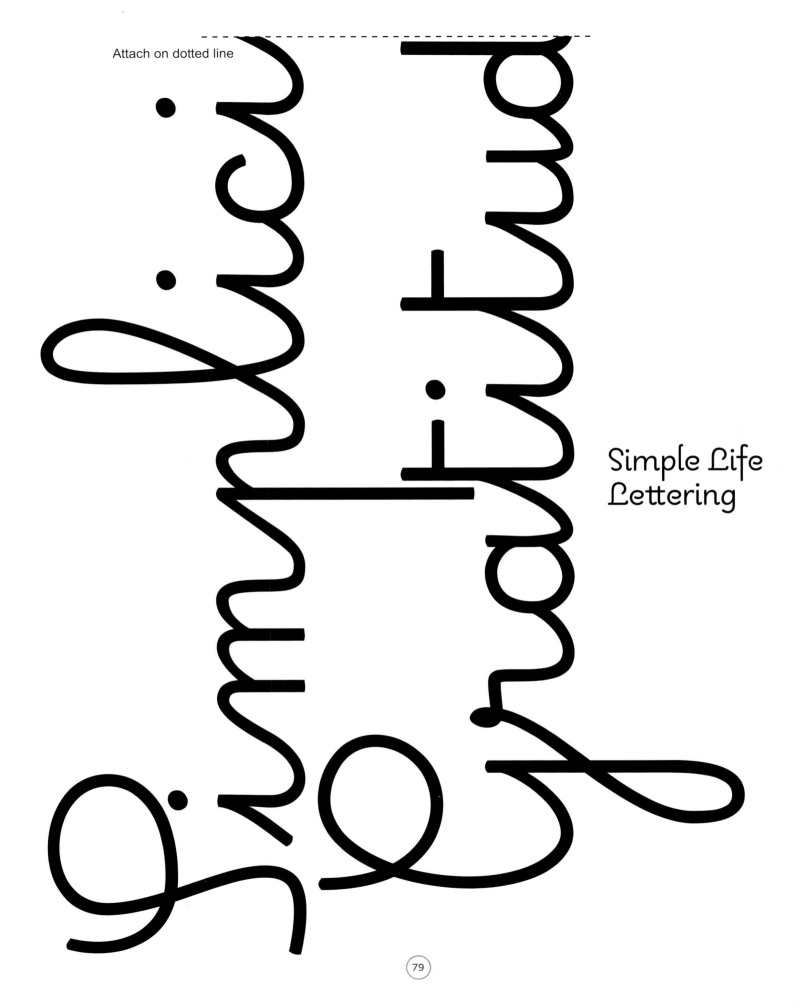

Attach on dotted line

Simple Life
Lettering

Attach on dotted line

Attach on dotted line

Attach on dotted line

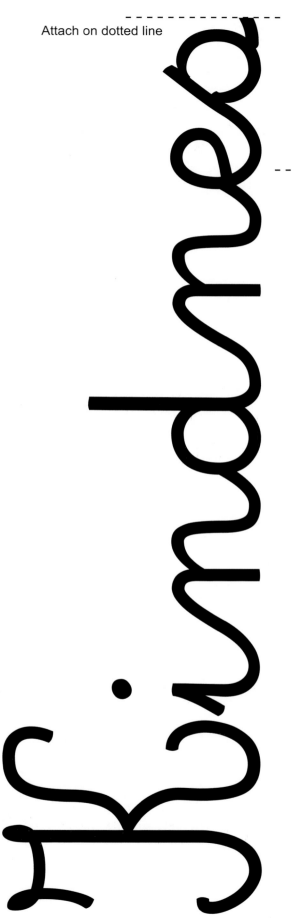

Kindness

party

Simple Life
Lettering

Welcome
Home
Wallhanging

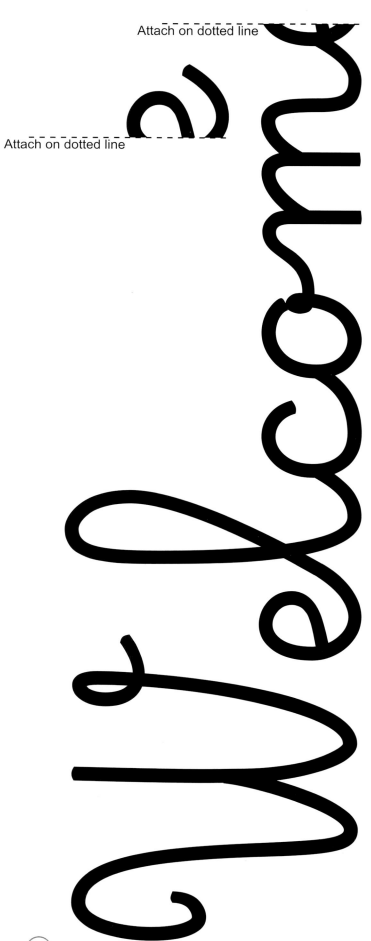

Give
Thanks
Runner
Lettering

8 Charming Children's Quilts and more

Story Time: Picture Quilts to Stir a Child's Imagination by Kim Gaddy contains eight charming quilts and a project with instructions to use it in various ways that will enchant the special young child in your life. With each quilt, Kim presents the idea behind it. The rest of the story is up to you and your child. What is the puppy doing? Is the bunny getting ready for bed? Will the cat catch a fish? These and other friendly characters go about their lives in a series of simply-pieced picture blocks. Some appliqué and embroidery are used to enhance the quilts. ✻ 8½ x 11 inches, softcover, full-color, 96 pages

Available at PickleDishStore.com, Kansas City Star Quilts online